CONNECTICUT

A Scenic Discovery

Best Wishes '89
Scott Associates

Published by
Foremost Publishers, Inc.
An affiliate of Yankee Publishing Inc.
Dublin, New Hampshire 03444

CONNECTICUT
A Scenic Discovery

Photographs and Text by Steve Dunwell

Produced by Foremost Publishers, Inc.

An affiliate of Yankee Publishing Inc.

Connecticut has taken both its name and its character from its waters. Glaciers scraped the hills, shaped the valleys, leveled the coastal plain and etched the shoreline. They left a landscape of surprising beauty that has nourished more than three centuries of culture and tradition.

For two decades before beginning this assignment I had looked at Connecticut through windows. I had seen the white needle steeples of hill-top colonial villages glistening in the distance. I had scanned the unrolling shoreline landscape. And, I had surveyed its panoramas border to border. While tantalized then, I had little chance to explore Connecticut until this assignment offered the opportunity to examine the state in detail.

I was drawn first to the miles of rivers and streams, the glowing forest pools, and the meandering marshes and coastal inlets. The true beauty of Connecticut is as delicate as the light reflecting off these varied bodies of water. There is the beauty of an opalescent fog surrounding a vintage whaler at anchor in Mystic harbor on an August morning, and the bright sunlight glancing off Long Island Sound while silhouetting the Thimble Islands. Connecticut is the poignance of Riga Falls cloaked in autumnal vapor, as well as the elegance of Kent Falls where each separate cataract catches a different light. It is the rich promise and possibility which draws a fly fisherman into a pool of Housatonic reflections. And it is the surprise of a still woodland pond waiting in the dim light of a Hammonasset forest, and the drama of the Farmington River raging through Satan's Kingdom gorge.

The Connecticut River nurtured early Indian settlements, Adriaen Block's first explorations, and the colony's first villages with her fertile banks. The ragged coastline provided a succession of perfect harbors, creating early maritime prosperity. Fast-running rivers along the eastern and western sides of the state powered industrial development — brass factories on the Naugatuck, cotton mills on the Quinebaug, and scores of others on every available waterfall in between. While only ninety miles long and fifty-five miles wide, this remarkable state has more than two hundred fifty miles of shoreline, over eight thousand miles of rivers and streams, and six thousand lakes and ponds. These symphonies of light and water charm the landscape.

As well, this state has been transformed by three hundred fifty years of Connecticut Yankee enterprise. It has encouraged the upright traditionalism of Thomas Hooker and Jonathan Edwards while enjoying the outrageous eccentricity of Mark Twain, P. T. Barnum, and William

Gillette. The Connecticut Yankee could be an independent farmer, an enterprising manufacturer, an ingenious inventor, a skilled metal worker, a gregarious executive, a reclusive lobsterman, or just about anything else. This accommodation of human diversity and talent has made the Constitution State one of the most thoroughly civilized states in the union.

Look to the rolling hills. The colonial village with its church facing a town hall or general store across the common is the most characteristic product of this democratic tradition. Proud of its heritage, Connecticut has preserved scores of variations on this theme, with each community a gem in its own right. View Washington, Pomfret and Norfolk. Stroll through Sharon, Cornwall or Brookfield Center. Each is unique, yet all share a common design. A spirit of restrained yet determined righteousness animates them all.

While the skylines of these villages are often limited to a single white church steeple, the larger towns affirm their diversity of beliefs by multiplying the steeples against their skies. Along New Haven's Temple Street three different bell towers rise up in a row, joined on the skyline by the ivy towers of Yale. Another trio of churches lines Main Street in New Milford. The moorish roofs of the Barnum Museum define the Bridgeport sky, as do the bold curves of

Landmark Plaza in Stamford and the richly detailed cornices of Town Hall in Norwich. This skyline pattern culminates at Hartford, where the gold-domed State House presides over a congregation of ancient churches and modern office towers with the onion-domed Colt Works for counterpoint.

From Canaan to Cos Cob, from Putnam to Pawcatuck, from Kent to Killingly, Connecticut presents a tapestry of exquisite detail. Often a small but perfect epiphany creates the most memorable experience: the quick movements of gloved hands adjusting tack before a horse show; the weathered grasp of a sea captain on the winch of his dragger; the effortless flick of a fisherman's wrist as he casts on the Salmon River; the rhythmic oar-strokes of a crew propelling their shell past Gales Ferry.

Nature provides an abundance of delicate moments and details. Blazing maple leaves brush their golden color onto the rough barn siding beside them. Mushrooms erupt from decaying logs in delightful asymmetry. Wildflowers and mountain laurel criss-cross the forest floor. Deer graze silently across abandoned twilight pastures.

What follows is the Connecticut I saw when I went through those early windows and submitted, without interference or distraction, to this state's subtle, delicate beauty; its grace and its power.

Boston, Mass.   Steve Dunwell
March, 1980

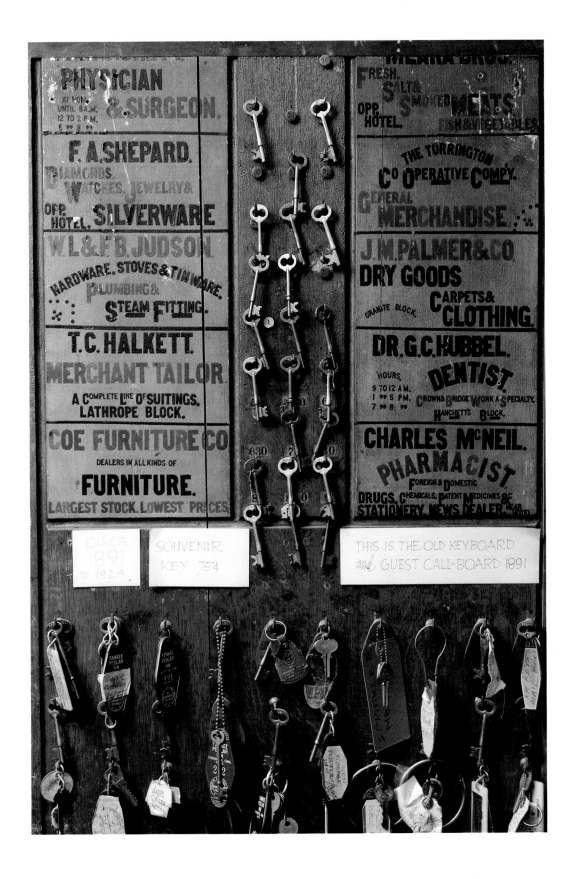

51. Floating in a Thimble Island haze, a lone fisherman waits.

52. Piccolo players practice "Yankee Doodle Dandy" before the Deep River Muster.

53. These musters are exhausting! Deep River.

54. This sway-backed farmhouse watches the valley above Lake Waramaug.

55. Apple harvest, Hawleyville.

56. A wildflower glows beside Mt. Riga's iron furnace.

57. Dandelions proclaim springtime in East Canaan.

58. Landmark Plaza divides the Stamford sky with pure geometry.

59. History marches along the cornice of Bridgeport's Barnum Museum.

60. October snow closes in on the Wentworth Homestead atop Mt. Riga.

61. Saturday night square dancing concludes the Harvest Festival at Kent.

62. A ray of sunlight isolates the Peirson College tower at Yale.

63. East Rock Park surveys New Haven from its steep palisades.

64. The rite of passage through Satan's Kingdom. Some make it. Some don't.

65. The Farmington River current pulls blithe inner tube riders into the Satan's Kingdom gorge.

66. A one-horse carriage trots between the oaks, Kent.

71. Historic homes flank the Congregational Church on Main Street, New Milford.

72. Dogwood blossoms remind Founders' Plaza of Spring, Hartford.

73. Sheer glass walls reflect Hartford's Center Church.

74. Yellow maples brush a barn on the Colebrook-Riverton road.

75. Ancient barn siding frames a boy in Pomfret.

76. East Canaan's church protects its hibernating valley in winter.

77. The gold-domed State House rules Hartford's Bushnell Park.

78. Brother and sister watch for minnows in the Mystic River.

79. The rising tide brings crabs towards the nets of these boys of Mystic.

80. Saturday morning haircut on Water St., Essex.

81. Mail in hand, a Colebrook villager strides from the post office to the general store.

82. Summer drought leaves Bull's Bridge hanging over the stony Housatonic riverbed below Kent.

83. October freshets flood the river while Bull's Bridge holds firm.

84. This pastoral panorama spreads to the horizon near New Milford.

85. Clouds pass a Housatonic ridge above West Cornwall.

86. Stony Creek harbor reaches out towards the Thimble Islands.

91. Sunset over the Thimble Islands, Stony Creek.

92. Tugboat pilot house, Essex.

93. Dragger winch and ropes, Stonington harbor.

94. Sunday morning in Washington brings in the congregation.

95. Three church spires delineate New Milford's Main Street.

96. Its silver-edged wake slicing the metallic calm, a powerboat heads out of Branford Harbor.

97. Fragile yet daring, a lone sailboat explores the silhouetted Thimble Islands.

98. Mushrooms erupt beside the trail to Cotton Hollow, Glastonbury.

99. Duet in progress, Kent Falls.

100. Spring tulips encircle City Hall, Hartford.

101. Riding into the sunset, a cyclist navigates Court Street, New Haven.

102. White snow on red leaves, Salisbury.

103. North Street snow scene, Litchfield.

104. Speed and poise combine as a carriage passes the Fairfield Hunt Club.

105. A final conference precedes the carriage driving event, Westport.

106. Sailors row homeward from their yacht across Sachem's Head harbor, Guilford.

111. The Chester-Hadlyme ferry scuttles across the Connecticut River in autumn haze.

112. Afternoon sun warms horses grazing at Tiffany Farm, North Lyme.

113. Acres of wildflowers spread across abandoned pastures in East Kent.

114. On a rainy Saturday, two girls plot to surprise historic Essex.

115. Would Dr. Hyde have approved?

116. Preparing for the draft horse pull, Goshen Fair.

117. Draft horse warm-up, Goshen Fair.

118. Thimble Island sunrise, from Brown Point, Branford.

WILLIAM HYDE . Senior
Physician ~ **1820**